These Hands

Written by Jamie Kleman
Illustrated by Elizabeth Shin

Copyright © 2016 Jamie Kleman

All rights reserved. No portion of this book may be used or reproduced in any manner whatsover without the express permission of the Publisher.

ISBN 13: 978-1533318169

ISBN 10: 1533318166

Written with much love for Abby and Will.
My hands and heart are here for you always.

-Mom

For Mom and her loving hands,
thank you for always being there for me...

-Elizabeth

This book is for:

_____

These handprints belong to:

_____

Trace your **left** hand on this page *with love.*

Trace your **right** hand on this page *with love.*

These hands count the days till you are born,
And hang the clothes that wait to be worn.

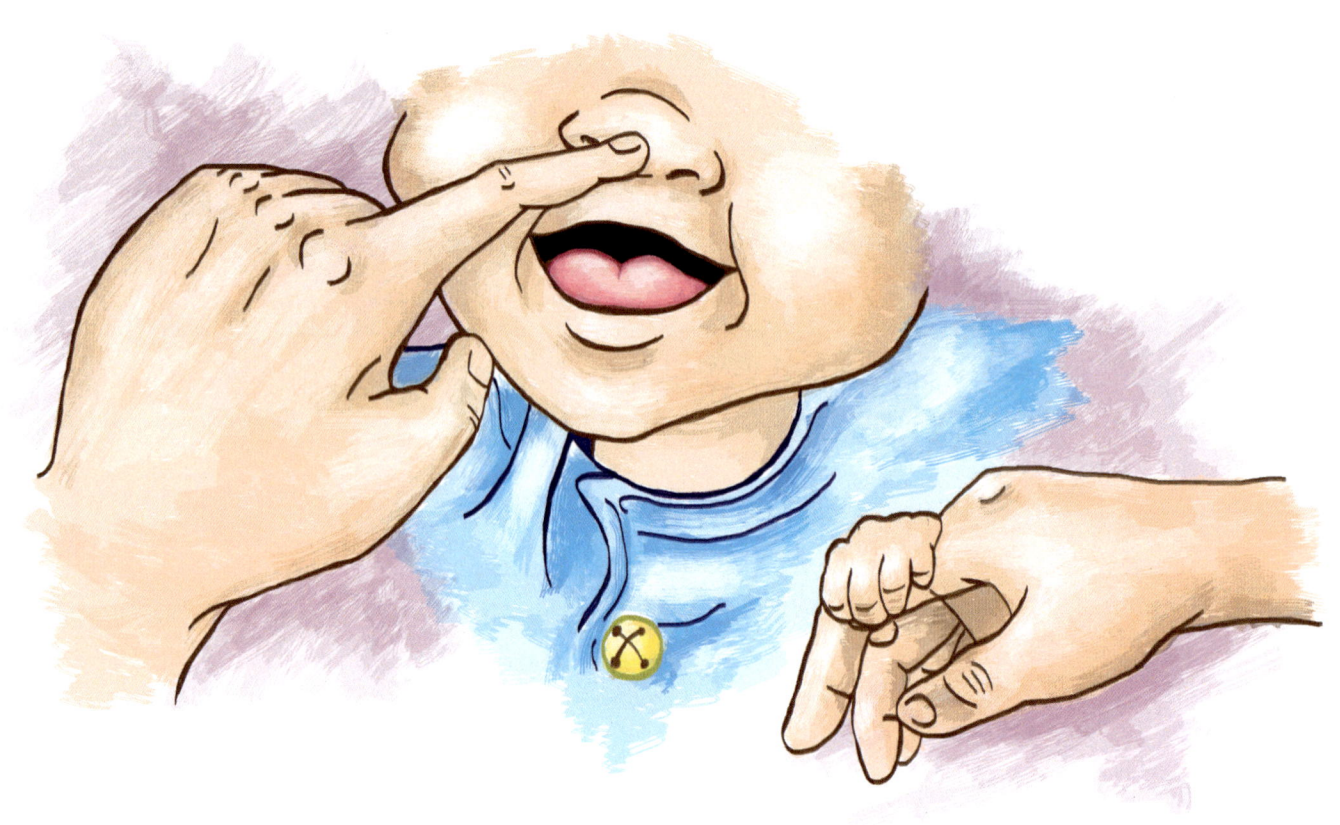

They wrap your fingers and tickle your toes.
They stroke your cheeks and beep your nose.

These hands pull you up as you learn to walk,
And read the books that help you talk.

They push the stroller each afternoon.
They point to the stars, the sun, and the moon.

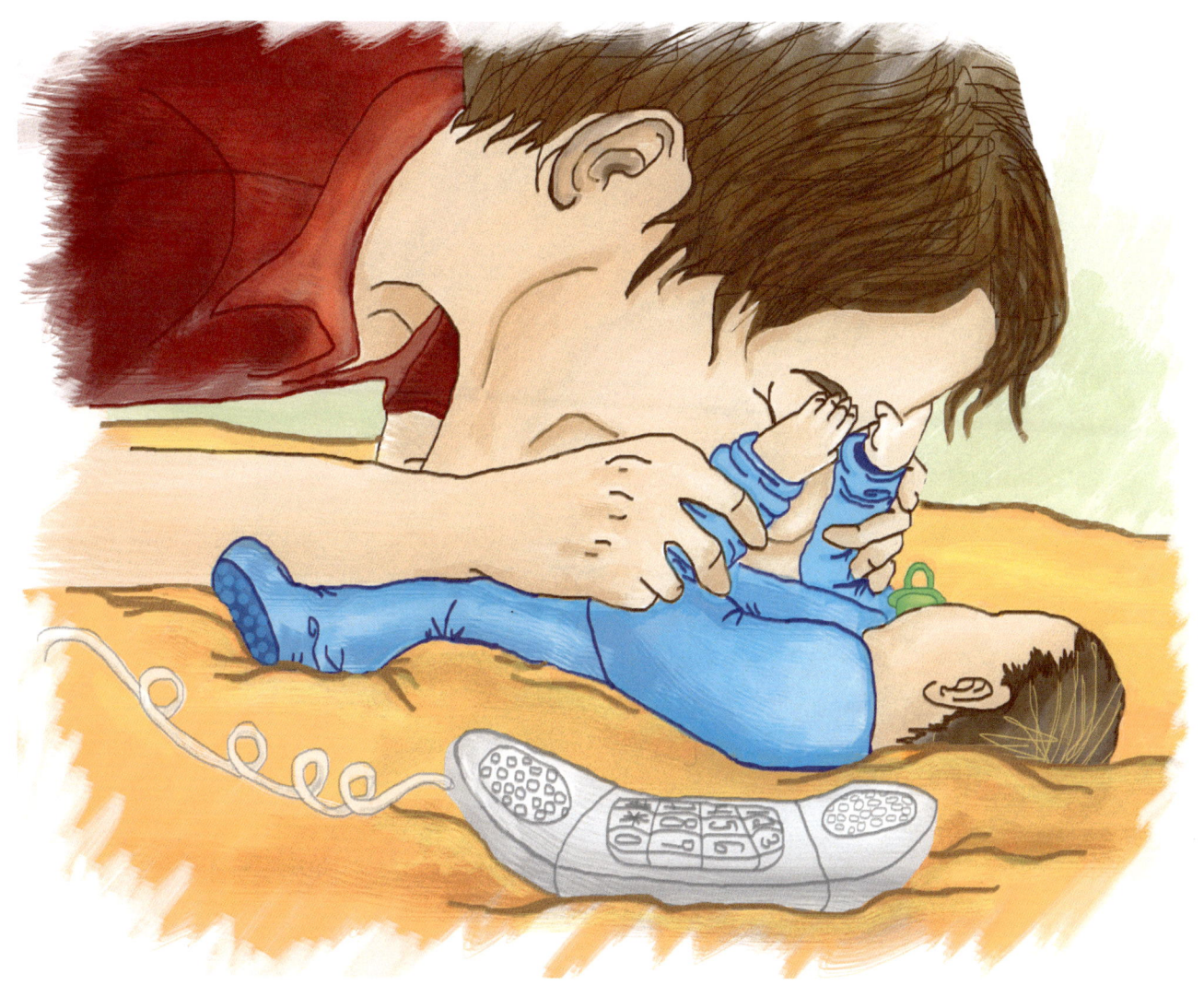

These hands play hours of peek-a-boo,
And make long calls to talk about you.

They tuck you in and kiss goodnight.
They hold you close and squeeze you tight.

These hands help you to climb up high,
And show you how to wave bye-bye.

They rub your tummy and heal hurt knees.
They set up picnics under trees.

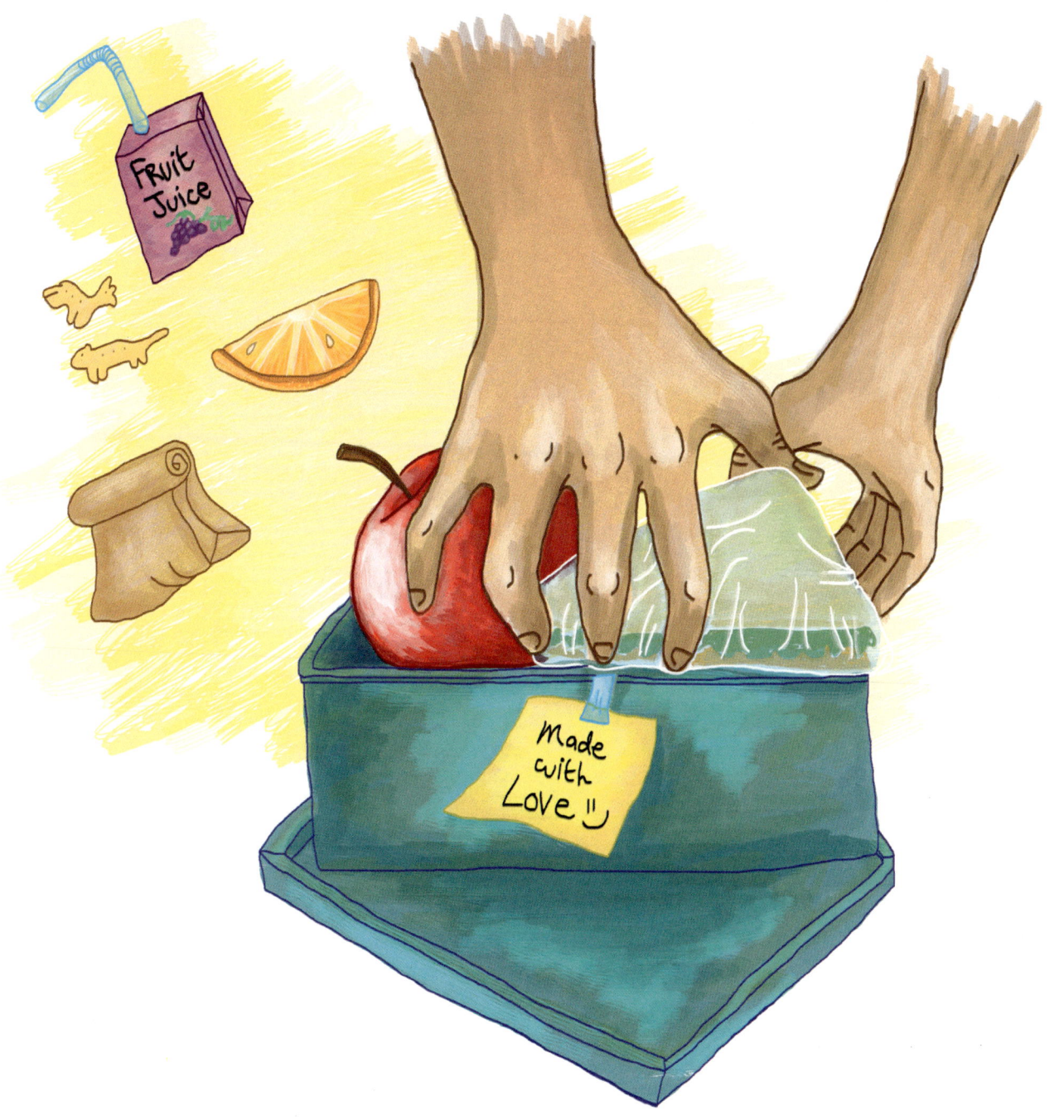

These hands pack snacks each day for school,
And catch you in the deep-end pool.

They clap with pride at every game—
Win or lose...it's all the same.

They pop popcorn for you and friends,
For sleepover fun that never ends.

These hands pat your back and give high-fives,
And pray real hard as you learn to drive.

These hands help pack as you leave the nest.
They write little notes wishing you the best.

They dry my eyes as you grow so tall,
Giving thanks that they were there for all.

These hands are here to pick up the phone,
And open the door when you come back home.

These are my hands to have and to hold,
For I love you more than can ever be told.

About the Author *Jamie Kleman*

At a very young age, Jamie Kleman fell in love with small books that conveyed big messages. She turned that love into a passion for writing stories and poetry for children.

Jamie lives in Pennsylvania with her husband, two children, and their pups. Her family is a constant source of love and support, and the inspiration they provide can be found on every page she writes.

About the Illustrator *Elizabeth Shin*

Elizabeth started doodling ever since she could remember, inspired by everything from Walt Disney to Shel Silverstein. She is very excited to be a part of Jamie's work to encourage and inspire children through her stories and poems.

Elizabeth is originally from North Carolina but currently resides in Delaware for graduate school.

Made in the USA
Columbia, SC
04 June 2022